LITTLE FLAG WAVE AT ME

Written by Yve Yakopovich

Illustrated by Melody Jeffries

For my little man, whose love of the American flag inspires us all!

Love, Mom
-YY

For my husband and our children, with all my love and gratitude.
This book is for you and the life we are building together.

Love, Mom
-MJ

Little flag, wave at me
On the lawn as I start the day

By the school
where children play
SCHOOL

In the morning light, for all to see

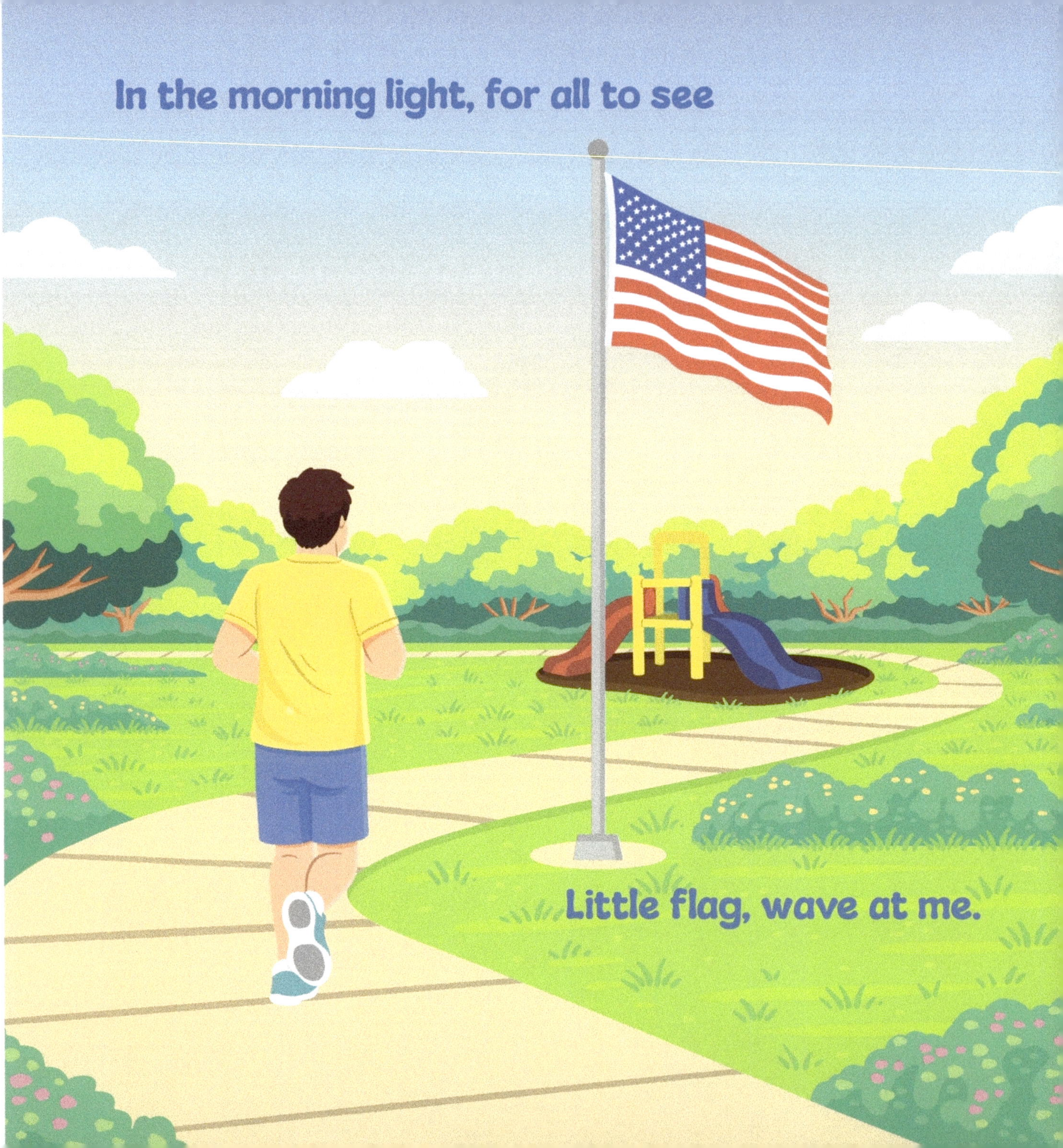

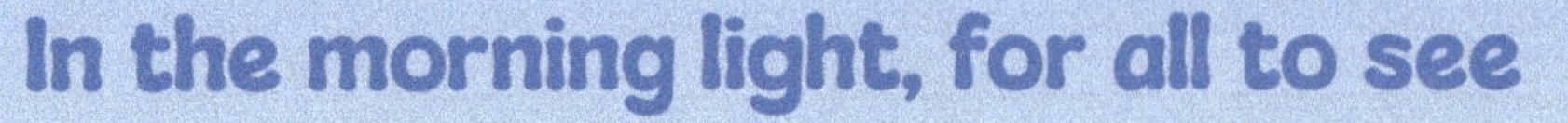

Little flag, wave at me.

Little flag, wave at me
LIBRARY
At the library where we read

At the community center,
watching over those in need
COMMUNITY CENTER
FRIDAY BINGO
6:00 PM

At the cafe while sipping tea
Little flag, wave at me.
BAKERY & CAFE

Little flag, wave at me

At the post office, where we send mail

At the military base,
as we say farewell

Little flag, wave at me.

Little flag, wave at me

At the ballpark, before the game

Outside the Players Hall of Fame

In the parade, fans smile with glee
Little flag, wave at me.

Little flag, wave at me

In the harbor waving high,
making ribbons in the sky

From a boat out at sea

Little flag, wave at me.

Little flag, wave at me
At the fort atop a hill

Where soldiers endured the winter chill

At every key moment
in our history

Little flag, wave at me.

Little flag, wave at me
At the memorial for those who died

From amber waves to crimson tide

For all who serve, brave and free
Little flag, wave at me.

Little flag, wave at me
While I picnic in the park,
as the sky turns to dark

From the mountains to the sea

Little flag, wave at me.

Little flag, wave at me

Atop the White House
lit up at night,

flowing with pride in pale moonlight

Saying goodnight
to you and me

Little flag, wave at me.

FLAG FACTS

The colors on the American flag symbolize valor (red), purity (white), and justice (blue)

Nicknames for the American flag include "Old Glory", "Stars and Stripes", "the Red, White, and Blue", and "the Star-Spangled Banner".

There is an American flag on the moon! But, it doesn't wave because there is no moving air.

The first flag was officially adopted by Congress on June 14, 1777 and only had 13 stars (states at the time) along with 13 stripes!

June 14 is now known as Flag Day to celebrate our flag.

www.ingramcontent.com/pod-product-compliance
Lightning Source LLC
Chambersburg PA
CBHW040220110726
48005CB00019B/3099